Croydo

TROLLEYBUSES

Terry Russell

Series editor Robert J Harley

MP Middleton Press

First published March 1996

ISBN 1 873793 73 1

© Middleton Press 1996

Design - Deborah Goodridge

Published by Middleton Press
        Easebourne Lane
        Midhurst
        West Sussex
        GU29 9AZ
        Tel: 01730 813169
        Fax: 01730 812601

Printed & bound by Biddles Ltd,
        Guildford and Kings Lynn

CONTENTS

INTRODUCTION AND ACKNOWLEDGEMENTS

I lived in Selhurst from 1934 to 1945. Compiling this book has brought back many memories of my young days spent, with my parents, in the Croydon area, so that it has been an absolute delight to undertake the task. The favourite pastime of one of my grand-mothers was to take me for a bus ride - upstairs, front seat. A day's outing to Putney for a towpath walk, included a long 630 trolleybus trip. My other grandmother lived near Addiscombe Station, which meant, 654 to either Spurgeons Bridge and a change to the irregular 59A bus, or to Goat House Bridge where we would pick up the very frequent 12 bus. For a shopping trip to Croydon we would take the 654 to West Croydon and transfer, using a special ticket, to the main road tram along North End to George Street. With a bit of luck, the day would end with a donkey ride in Kennard's Arcade. What would today's Health and Safety people think of that I wonder?

In 1945 we moved to "The Holy City" of Selsdon. This was the cry of the irreverent Catford based conductors of the route 54 bus. I attended Archbishop Tenison's Grammar School in South Croydon, and even when I married, only moved to Purley. So the local trams and trolleybuses were part of everyday life.

Many of the well known tramway photo-graphers took less interest in the replacement trolleybuses. I have, therefore, brought in the work of relatively unknown enthusiasts. Apart from my own pictures, I have made use of the work of my long standing friends, Derek Norman and Roy Hubble. Equally I have used the work of established photographers, Dr.Hugh Nicol, John Meredith, John Gent, D.A.Thompson, Geoff Baddeley and John Price.

I have also drawn from the photographic collections of Mike Skeggs and Robert Harley, to obtain shots individually credited in the text. "So-and-so's collection"! appears all too often as a credit these days, but as so many prints were sold with nothing on the back, then sadly, this is the only recourse. So if I have not made the correct credit, that is the reason and I apologise most sincerely.

My thanks to my son Keith and to Geoff Smith for producing such excellent prints from the original negatives of John Price and myself. Such a skill is not found easily in 1996.

The London Trolleybus Preservation Society (LTPS) is doing marvellous work, preserving London trolleybuses at the East Anglia Transport Museum at Carlton Colville near Lowestoft in Norfolk. The book *Trolley-bus* written by Ken Blacker, one of the Museum's driving forces, and Michael Dryhurst's *London Trolleybus* have been a mine of information, especially for the vehicle details. My own scale drawing is included, as modellers are finding it more and more difficult to obtain such information. If the tramcar pictures bring a desire for more, I would direct the reader to the companion Middleton Press album *Croydon's Tramways* which completes the history of road bound electric public transport in the Croydon area.

Traffic notices and other London Transport publications are reproduced by permission of London Transport Museum.

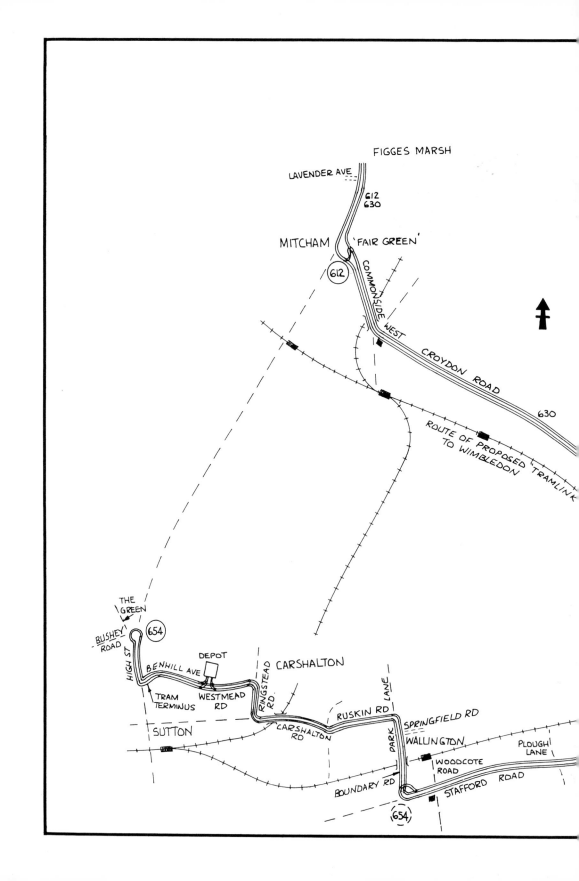

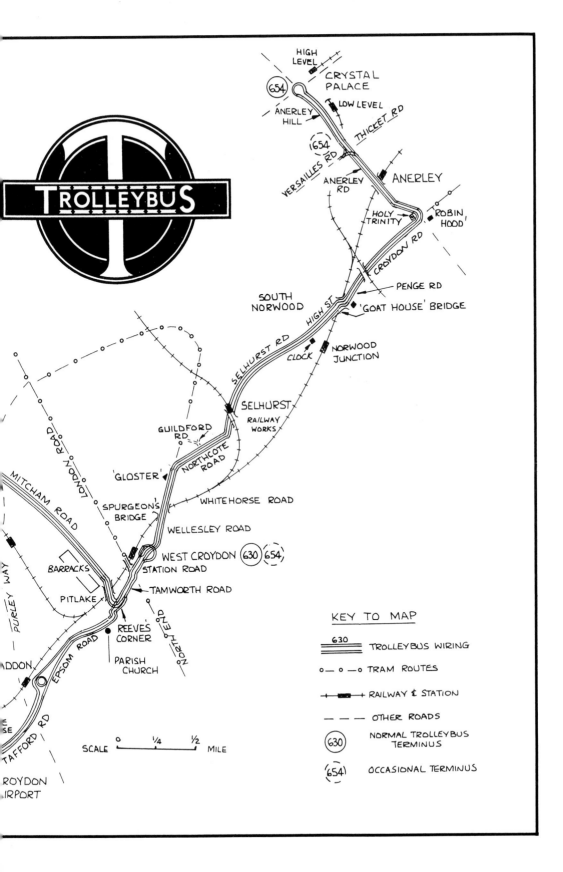

GEOGRAPHICAL SETTING

Croydon is about 10 miles/16kms south of London. The original settlement grew up just north of an important gap with a series of deep dry valleys through the chalk of the North Downs. These hills reach their highest point, 882ft./268 metres above sea level some 7 miles/11kms to the south. To the north are the Norwood Hills which reach a height of 376ft./114 metres above sea level. To the east of the town the Addington Hills consist of undulating heath and woodland, whilst to the west, it is generally flatter and low lying around streams which form the source of the River Wandle, which flows north to the River Thames at Wandsworth.

HISTORICAL BACKGROUND

Commencing early in this century, the routes covered by this album were operated as electric tramways by the South Metropolitan Electric Tramway and Lighting Company, jointly with Croydon Corporation Tramways. The section west of Croydon was a shared operation, while the remainder was SMET entirely. From 1933, the public road transport of the area was administered by the London Passenger Transport Board (LPTB). One of their first tasks was to rid the streets of a grossly outdated mode of transport - the open top tramcar. Sights were set on the two worst areas, Woolwich to Dartford (covered in the companion Middleton Press volume on that area), and the routes running east and west from Croydon. The main tram route to London was earmarked for modernisation later in 1942, but the Second World War put a stop to that.

In many ways, the 654 trolleybus service was non-standard, compared with what the LPTB would introduce over the following four years. The B1 type vehicles were one bay shorter than No. 62, already deemed to be the "Standard" for the Capital. The elegantly designed side-bracket overhead support brackets (known as "bowstrings") were used in large quantities in this area. Even the route number did not reflect the later trend to add 500 or 600 to the tram route number. The reason for this non-conformity was that 604 and 605 were already in use in the Kingston area.

The route ran from the centre of Croydon to the north-east, through narrow, long estab-lished, working class, residential districts, to the London County Council boundary along-side South London's playground - the Crystal Palace. This enormous, impressive building, designed by William Paxton, started life as the Main Hall of the 1851 Exhibition situated in Hyde Park in the heart of London. It was moved later to the Anerley site, bounded by pleasure gardens and water features.

In the opposite, south-westerly direction, after passing Croydon Old Town and the grand Parish Church, it then served mainly residen-tial areas developed during the late 1920s and 1930s. It ran past parks and mansions to the country town of Sutton - a world away from smokey Norwood or Anerley.

Initially it was completely isolated from the rest of the London trolleybus network, but in 1937 a long tentacle reached out across Mitcham Common and made it part of the whole. However this changed nothing; the initial batch of buses remained for the duration of the service and only strayed at Christmas.

Through this volume we will ride the 654 from Sutton to Crystal Palace, and then the 630 from West Croydon to just beyond the Croydon County boundary in Mitcham.

When the proposed *Croydon Tramlink* system comes into being at the end of the century, it will traverse certain thoroughfares formally covered by the trolleybuses, namely Tamworth and Station Roads. Once again the town will be served by smooth riding, swift, pollution free, electric public transport!

Route 654 Sutton to Crystal Palace
SUTTON

1. Resplendent in their new uniforms the driver and conductor stand in front of 89 prior to the 51 minute journey to Crystal Palace in the Spring of 1936. Listed below the stop sign are the points served by the route. (A.D.Packer)

981.—WHITE CAP COVERS AND WHITE COATS.

The staff are reminded that White Cap Covers must be worn continuously from May 1st to September 30th. White Coats (Trolleybus Drivers) must be worn from June 1st to September 30th, and may be worn in May.

From LT traffic circular April 1936

2. Early into the Second World War we see 78 at Sutton terminus. The buses are still in their "as built" condition, but wartime blackout regulations have been instigated. Headlamps have been heavily masked and white paint has been applied to the front mudguards and side lifeguard slats. The roofs were to remain silver for a little longer. Black and white stripes have also been applied to just about every stationary object in the street too! The Wrigleys advert says that chewing gum is "Wartime first aid", they didn't miss a trick did they? (Charles F. Klapper)

3. The turning circle at Bushey Road, Sutton was very tight and only one bus could stand at the boarding point. Trolleybus 79 awaits departure time, while 90 pulls out of Bushey Road into the High Street. (R.J.Harley Coll.)

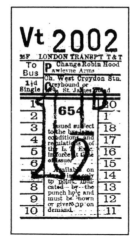

PJ 9286

25 A #L. T. Trolleybuses

P	Ch'ge Robin Hood Pawleyne Arms	20
Chg	Grapes, Sutton Chancer Road or Sutton Station	19
C		18
Ang	Change Grapes or Bushey Rd. Sutton	17
		16
C	Ch'ge W. Croydon Sn Greyhound or St.	16
R	Deer James Rd	15
S	Swan and Sugar Loaf	14
		13
1	654	12
2		11
3		10
4	For conditions see back	9
5		8
6	1½d., 2d. 1d. Child	7

TO BUS

Vt 2002

2F LONDON TRANSPT T & T

To Bus	P	Change Robin Hood Pawleyne Arms
	Ch.	West Croydon Stn.
1½d Single	C	Greyhound or St. James Road

1			20
2	654		1
3		Issued subject to the bye-laws conditions and regulations of the L. T. in force at time of issue. Available on date issued only to point indicated by the punch hole and must be shown or given up on demand.	18
4			17
5			16
6			15
			14
8			13
9			12
10			11

250 1½d Ord. 654 Rev

| To Bus | A | Ch. Grapes, Sutton Alexandra Avenue or Sutton Station |
| | A | ChGr'pe sor Bushey Rd Angel Sutton |

For transfer journeys only **one** change is allowed which must be made at indicated point to **next available tram or bus**. **Not transferable.**

4. Approaching the terminus at the lower end of Sutton High Street on a dull February day, just a month before the final run. (R.Hubble)

6. Ex South Metropolitan Electric Tramways (SMET) car 2S stands at the terminus in Benhill Road, Sutton under the new trolleybus wiring in late 1935. Other views of this terminus in tram days are included in the Middleton Press volume *Croydon's Tramways*. As there was no road space for the turning circle required by the replacement trolleybuses, a half mile extension was built to the right along the High Street to Bushey Road, often referred to as The Green. (G.N.Southerden)

5. No.69 makes the tight turn from the High Street into Benhill Road. The silver painted fluted overhead support poles, specified by Sutton Council, are seen in the High Street and the standard, green LPTB type can be spotted behind the lady tending her baby in its shaded perambulator. (C.Carter)

7. On a fine winter's day 492 passes a row of typical 1930s suburban houses in Benhill Avenue. (A.B.Cross)

8. Both milk and people are being delivered by electricity as 91 speeds into Benhill Avenue on a day requiring the shop blind to be lowered to protect the goods on display from the sun. (C.Carter)

9. Trams and trolleybuses were housed in depots, whilst omnibuses belonged in garages. In 1950 all such establishments were grouped together and Sutton Depot became Carshalton Garage in November to prevent duplication of names. While the crews of 81 change over, fellow drivers get tuition on RT 5 prior to the conversion. I gave the crews a cine film show in the upstairs canteen. They were delighted to see the results of one of the cameramen who had been filming them during the final months. (R.J.Harley Coll.)

10. The depot yard hosts trolleys 75 and 76, plus RT 277 spilling out from the overcrowded Sutton bus garage. Carshalton Depot provided 21 trolleybuses on weekdays and 26 on Saturday solely to the 654 service. (D.A.Thompson)

11. Access to London Transport premises was usually very restricted, but towards the end it became more relaxed. No.78 is on the space-saving, traversing turntable. It was controlled by old tramcar equipment and the warning gong is now on the preserved Class E1 tramcar at the National Tramway Museum in Derbyshire, thanks to the filmshow!
(Terry Russell)

13. An interior view of 78 looking towards the rear loading platform shows the double sided, red, blue and gold *Trolleybus* motif on the rear window. On the left-hand bulkhead is a casement containing the farechart.
(Terry Russell)

12. Out in the yard we see the driver of 87 using the bamboo pole to place the power collecting trolleypoles on the overhead wires. Dewired poles have taken their toll on the asbestos sheet cladding of the shed. (Terry Russell)

14. The driver has placed 84 in the correct position at the top of Ringstead Road ready to make the turn into Carshalton Road.
(D.A.Thompson)

WALLINGTON

15. On a sunny February day 491 coasts round the corner from Park Lane into Ruskin Road, Wallington on its way to Sutton. Up the hill to the right is where trolleys on test from Sutton Depot reversed. They would stop on the hill, pull the poles down, back by gravity into Springfield Road, roll back out into Park Lane, put the poles up and run back to base. (Terry Russell)

16. Looking from the opposite direction, 81 follows a motorcyclist out into Park Lane in late February 1959. (Terry Russell)

FIRST & LAST TROLLEYBUSES   On & after May 17, 1953

ROUTE 654 | Sutton - Wallington - Croydon - Crystal Palace | P.M. times are in heavy figures

Via Sutton High Street, Benhill Avenue, Lower Road, Westmead Road, Ringstead Road, Carshalton Road, Ruskin Road, Park Lane, Stanley Park Road, Stafford Road, Epsom Road, Waddon Road, Tamworth Road, Station Road, Wellesley Road, Whitehorse Road, Northcote Road, South Norwood High Street, Penge Road, Croydon Road, Anerley Road

RAILWAY STATIONS SERVED : Wallington, Waddon, West Croydon, Selhurst, Norwood Junction, Anerley, Crystal Palace

Service interval : WEEKDAYS 4-5 mins., SUNDAY morning 8 mins., afternoon and evening 5 mins.

	WEEKDAYS First	MON. to FRI. Last	SATURDAY Last	SUNDAY First	SUNDAY Last
SUTTON *Bushey Road*	¶ 5 39	10 43 11 24 12 24 ..	10 42 11 24 12 26	.... 8 23	10 43 11 24 12 27
Carshalton *LT Garage*	4 48 5 17 5 44 ..	10 48 11 29 12 29	10 47 11 29 12 31	8 5 8 28 ..	10 48 11 29 12 32
Stanley Park Road *Woodcote Road*	4 58 5 27 5 54	10 58 11 39	10 57 11 39 ...	3 15 8 38	10 58 11 39 ....
West Croydon *Station*	†5 14 5 40 6 7 ..	11 11 11 52 ..	11 11 11 53 ..	8 28 8 51	11 11 11 52 ..
Anerley *Robin Hood*	5 29 5 55 6 22	11 26	11 26	8 43 9 6 ...	11 26 ....
CRYSTAL PALACE *White Swan*	5 36 6 2 6 29 ..	11 33 ..	11 33 ...	8 50 9 13 ..	11 33 ....
CRYSTAL PALACE *White Swan*	.... 5 38 6 4	11 40	11 40 ...	.... ¶	8 32 11 35 ...
Anerley *Robin Hood*	.. 5 45 6 11 ..	11 47 ..	11 47 ...	..	8 39 11 42 ..
West Croydon *Station*	.. 6 0 6 26 ...	12 2 ..	12 2 ...	8 13 8 47	8 54 11 57 ..
Stanley Park Road *Woodcote Road*	.. 6 13 6 39 ...	12 15	12 16 ...	8 26 9 0	9 7 12 10 ..
Carshalton *LT Garage*	5 30 6 23 6 49 ...	12 25	12 26 ...	8 16 8 36 9 10	9 17 12 20 ..
SUTTON *Bushey Road*	5 35 6 28 6 54 ..	12 30	12 31 ...	8 21 8 41 9 15	9 22 12 25 ..

SPECIAL SUNDAY JOURNEYS

Sutton *Bushey Road* to Crystal Palace at 7 40 a.m.   Boundary Road to West Croydon at 7 57 a.m.
Carshalton *LT Garage* to Crystal Palace at 6 28 a.m.   Crystal Palace to Carshalton *LT Garage* at 7 15 a.m.
Carshalton *LT Garage* to West Croydon at 7 15 a.m.   West Croydon to Boundary Corner at 7 42 a.m.

¶—Special early journey.   †—Arrives at 5 11 a.m.

17. The turning circle at Boundary Road, Wallington was only used early on Sunday morning. The destination on 89 is the only example, other than the two route end displays that I have found on film. This odd working can be followed on the adjacent timetable. Thankfully for us, Derek Norman got up early on that Sunday. (D.Norman)

18. Sutton bound 81 turns from Stanley Park Road into Boundary Road with the turning circle on its right. (R.J.Harley Coll.)

19. In Wallington, on the corner of the Stafford and Woodcote Road crossing, was the Test Centre where your author passed his motorcycle driving test, thus enabling the Trolley chasing to go on. No.79 passes by on its way to Croydon. (D.Norman)

WADDON

20. While the Southern Railway personnel are being athletic at their grounds in Plough Lane adjacent to Croydon Airport, 1050 speeds silently along Stafford Road. Trolleybuses were not called *Silent Death* for nothing. The other appendages to the traction pole are worthy of note, especially the dated gas street light. (E.W.Crawforth)

21. On 7th February 1959 in Stafford Road, 86 has retired from active service with a problem. Trolleypoles are stowed under the hooks while the crew smoke in the lower saloon awaiting the arrival of the breakdown tender from Sutton depot. The bamboo retriever has been left resting against the rear dome. It was carried in a long steel tube underneath the bus. Access was from the rear, below the U.S.Royal tyre advertisement. (R.Hubble)

22. On the penultimate day, 93 pulls away from The Chase stop in Stafford Road. The factories behind were part of the Croydon Airport industrial estate which contained such well known manufacturers as Bowaters, Philips, Mullards, Rollasons and Louis Newmark's where I worked for 10 years and met the other love of my life! (R.Hubble)

23. My rather flamboyant Aunt Connie, wife of a 1930s bandleader, lived in "The Ridgeway", Waddon, which meant that the Waddon Station stop was used on my visits from Selhurst. No.84 cannot pull into the kerb as Rickett Cockerell's coal delivery lorry is parked outside their office. (A.B.Cross)

24. Waddon Station boasted an unconnected circle of wires and a place on the destination blind, but I never saw it used in real time or photographically. No.67 takes us home after a visit to Auntie Connie. (D.A.Thompson)

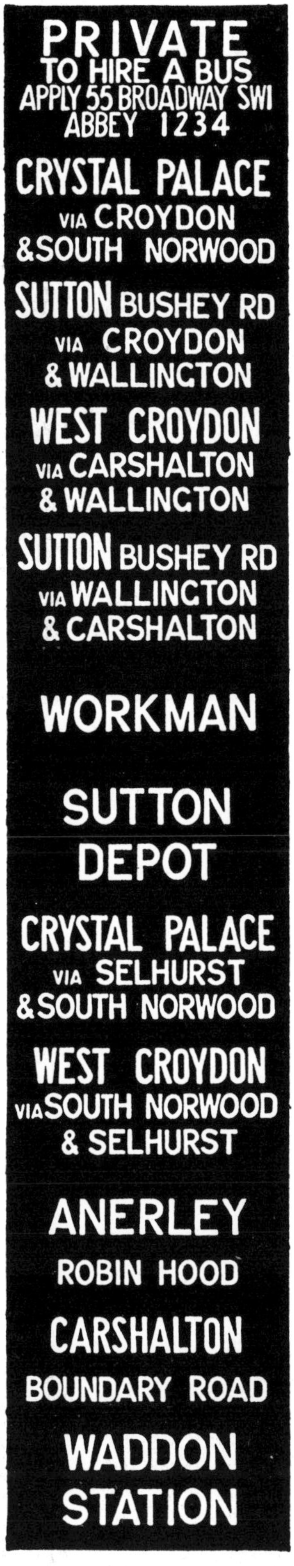

PRIVATE
TO HIRE A BUS
APPLY 55 BROADWAY SW1
ABBEY 1234

CRYSTAL PALACE
VIA CROYDON
&SOUTH NORWOOD

SUTTON BUSHEY RD
VIA CROYDON
& WALLINGTON

WEST CROYDON
VIA CARSHALTON
& WALLINGTON

SUTTON BUSHEY RD
VIA WALLINGTON
& CARSHALTON

WORKMAN

**SUTTON
DEPOT**

CRYSTAL PALACE
VIA SELHURST
&SOUTH NORWOOD

WEST CROYDON
VIA SOUTH NORWOOD
& SELHURST

ANERLEY

ROBIN HOOD

CARSHALTON

BOUNDARY ROAD

**WADDON
STATION**

**EXTRA
654**

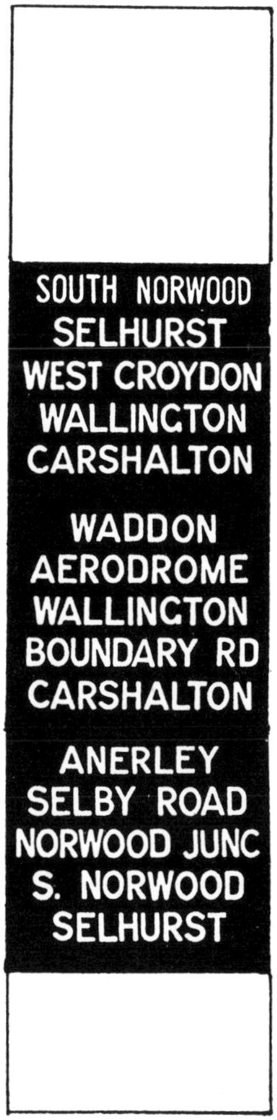

SOUTH NORWOOD
SELHURST
WEST CROYDON
WALLINGTON
CARSHALTON

WADDON
AERODROME
WALLINGTON
BOUNDARY RD
CARSHALTON

ANERLEY
SELBY ROAD
NORWOOD JUNC
S. NORWOOD
SELHURST

25. "Ladders-light, ladders-long, ladders-stout, ladders-strong, made and sold by Philpott John, Waddon Road, Croydon", so read the notice out of view near the woodyard on the left. Behind the yard is the railway to Sutton which features in Middleton Press album *West Croydon to Epsom.* (D.Norman)

26. A Sutton bound trolley passes the fine Croydon Parish Church in Old Town. The granite drinking trough for horses on the right is also nearing the end of its required life. "Gilbert's meat pies" were made in the shop on the left and their contents were always the subject of much schoolboy humour! (D.Norman)

REEVE'S CORNER

27. Reeve's Corner was so called because Messrs. E. Reeves, Auctioneers, House furnishers and Ironmongers, occupied many of the shops at this point. The temporary car park was a bombsite still not built on since the 1940s. No.73 passes a green, country area RT on its way to Sutton. (Pamlin Prints)

880.—ROUTE No. 654—MINISTRY OF TRANSPORT REGULATIONS.

Notice to Trolleybus Drivers.

The following maximum speeds must be strictly observed :—

30 miles an hour.
In Stafford Road, Stanley Park Road, Boundary Road, Park Lane and Ruskin Road.

25 miles an hour.
In Epsom Road, Carshalton Park Road, Beynon Road, Carshalton Road, Ringstead Road, Westmead Road, Lower Road and Benhill Avenue.

20 miles an hour.
In Station Road (Croydon), Tamworth Road, Church Street, St. John's Road, Waddon Road, Benhill Street and High Street (Sutton).

10 miles an hour.
In Elis David Place and Elis David Road.
When passing from Station Road (Croydon) into Tamworth Road and *vice versa*.
When rounding the turns between the following, in either direction :—
(a) Stanley Park Road and Boundary Road.
(b) Park Lane and Ruskin Road.
(c) Carshalton Road and Ringstead Road.
(d) Ringstead Road and Westmead Road.
(e) Lower Road and Benhill Avenue.
(f) Benhill Street and High Street (Sutton).

5 miles an hour.
When rounding all turning circles and when passing under junctions or crossings in the overhead wires.

From LT traffic circular February 1936

28. The Parish Church provides the backdrop as a 654 and Wallington bound country area green RT 4250 pass in Church Street. From here to Sutton the trolleybus shared little of its route with other competing services.
(Terry Russell)

29. Trips to Harts, the Butchers in Church Street (possibly on 85) for my bus riding grandmother, plus the fact that my grandfather was Manager of Reeve's office furniture department on the centre island, ensured many trolleybus journeys to Reeve's Corner, or as the conductors called it- "Spredeegle". The pub on the corner was The Spread Eagle!
(D.A.Thompson)

30. Here the 630 route from Mitcham joined the 654 for the final part of its run to West Croydon. Vertical wires were strung between the traction poles level with Baldwins the Butchers upper floor windows. These prevented a dewired trolleypole from entering the bedroom! The unusual overhead wire configuration on the Sutton bound line was an unsuccessful experiment to control the overhead points by the driver from his cab. The hood on the pole above the rear dome of 72, houses the signal for single line working by the 630s in Lower Church Street to the left.
(D.A.Thompson)

TROLLEYBUS OVERHEAD EQUIPMENT

Improved Route Selection

AN electric induction device is being tested by the London Passenger Transport Board to enable trolleybus overhead wire frogs at junctions to be set from the driver's cab. One of the difficulties has hitherto been the speedy operation of junctions and turning points which provide for the routeing of vehicles. These were at first all hand-operated, and the conductor had to remain at the operating point until the bus had passed through the junction. Later, experiments were carried out with a system by which the route was selected according to whether the driver motored or coasted over a selected section of the line. The objection to this was that control of the vehicle was interfered with at perhaps the most important points on the road.

Later, a system was designed and installed at many turnouts by which the path for the bus was determined by pressing a button attached to a standard in rear of the junction, wiring being duplicated for some distance where necessary. The action of pressing the button not only selected the road, but the junction in the wires was locked in the correct position until the bus had passed a contactor on the overhead equipment. A further device on the principle of electric induction has now been introduced by London Transport engineers which does away with any necessity for the conductor to leave the platform at all. A time-delayed switch is installed in the driver's cab, connected to an induction coil mounted on the roof, and with this he is able to select the correct road and to retain full control of the bus while passing through busy junctions. Experimental equipment has been installed at West Croydon, where the two routes to Mitcham and Sutton diverge, and one trolleybus (No. 90) at Sutton depot has been equipped with the necessary gear. Further installations will be put in if the present one is found successful.

(Reproduced from Modern Transport)

32. Soon after the introduction of the 630, No. 435 is seen turning from Tamworth Road into Lower Church Street. The Eagle Pub stands in its original roadside position, later to be demolished and the pavement widened but not the roadway! For many years a one way system was proposed for Reeve's Corner but the relocation of the trolleybus wiring was always the reason for its rejection.
(C.F.Klapper)

31. Why 90 is showing EXTRA instead of 654 is a mystery. When photographing at the Crystal Palace terminus, I persuaded a conductor to put up EXTRA, as I had never seen it displayed. Having done it for me, the conductor forgot(!) and the bus went on its way to Croydon. I have often wondered how far it got before an irate inspector chastised the poor chap. (C.Carter)

WEST CROYDON

33. In tram days the SMET Sutton cars terminated at the top of Tamworth Road, hence the name of the cafe. The yellow paper sticker on the pole outside announces that next week, 69 will be replaced by an RT bus on route 154 or 157 in Stage 1 of the London Transport trolleybus to bus conversion scheme. (C.Carter)

⟶

34. The unusual advertisement on 89 takes our eye, while Moores Presto Motor Works has ceased trading. Dialling CRO 6004 will not discover the price of Simonise wax car polish. Class D2, 467 loads behind on route 630. (C.Carter)

⟶

35. Saturday shoppers in January 1959 wait for the traffic lights to change to North End/London Road at West Croydon. No.79 in the past would have been crossing the tracks of LT tram routes 16, 18 and 42 at this point. Surprisingly no photograph has come to light of this interesting meeting of two forms of electric traction. (J.E.Gready)

36. Ex Croydon Corporation E1 class tram 391 unloads outside John Bright's Jewellers where I bought my wife's wedding ring. This the nearest I can get to that elusive picture - there is a trolleybus traction pole outside the tobacconists ahead of the tram! (J.B.Gent)

37. In Station Road, West Croydon, the 654 stop was ahead of the 630. Both services leave for Sutton and Harlesden respectively. A spectacular dewirement occurred here when a 630 driver pulled out to pass a loading 654. The trolleys of the 630 ran down the back of the 654's poles and then took to the air! The *Trolleybus* motif on the rear window was there, as a reminder, to prevent such an error. (R.Hubble)

38. During September 1958, Class J3, 1049-51 were needed to replace Sutton's flood damaged B1s. They were fitted with run-back brakes but as they were standard 30 foot vehicles, not "Shorties", they were driven by volunteers. No.1050 picks up passengers outside the Creamery Restaurant in Station Road. (M.Skeggs Coll.)

39. When the 654 service started in 1936, some ex London United Tramways class A1 "Diddler" trolleybuses were used until the delivery of sufficient class B1s. As no photographs have come to light, the next best thing is this shot of No.7 on route 630 learner duties at West Croydon. (LTPS)

40. An ex SMET tram 38S stands at the West Croydon terminus of the Crystal Palace section in late 1935. The metal Spencer hoops at the end of the upper deck were to protect passengers from a falling trolley boom. As these are still in place, it indicates that trolleybus wiring has not yet been erected under Selhurst Station railway bridge. However, a new green tubular pole has been planted outside what was originally The Station Picture Hall, Croydon's first cinema in 1908. (R.Hubble Coll.)

41. It is now January 1936. The trolleybus wiring at Selhurst has been erected, Spencer hoops have been removed from the tram, and the West Croydon to Sutton tram service converted to trolleybuses. Brand new 73 is seen on the right. What a marvellous transition for the travelling public. Now passengers, drivers and conductors all get a warm and dry ride! (E.G.P.Masterman)

42. Waiting in the queue to go home in Station
Road, West Croydon! Two trolleys have gone
off full with five standing, but on 491 there is
room downstairs for us on the long bench seat
over the rear wheels. (Terry Russell)

43. A wonderful, action packed scene as
shoppers scramble aboard 74 in Station Road
on the last Saturday. As schedules ran
Wednesday to Tuesday, the final run will be in
three days time. (Terry Russell)

44. Not so busy on 14th February 1959. After 87 has moved off, the conductor of the 630 behind will have to set the overhead points for the terminal stand, using the control box on the right hand traction pole. (Pamlin Prints)

45. No.69 on the early Sunday morning journey from Boundary Road terminates at deserted West Croydon. The bin contained sand for icy turning circles. The 64 bus route would be unsuccessfully extended to replace part of both the 654 and the 630 routes in the future. (D.Norman)

46. Top deck, front seats were the favourite! A 630 turns at the bottom of St. Michaels Road, while the driver of our 654 awaits "two on the bell" from his conductor. RTs, both red 75 and green 409 and 411, await departure time. (R.Hubble)

47. The Luftwaffe took exception to the estate agents and the houses on the right, but it did clear the site in readiness for the new bus station. The taxi seems in a frightful rush as 73 slows for the overhead crossings. (L.Rowe)

Frogs, Crossings and Section Insulators

The speed of trolleybuses under frogs and crossings must not exceed 5 m.p.h.

Drivers must pass under all insulated crossings and section insulators with the power pedal in the "**off**" position, the power pedal being allowed to return quickly to this position. Failure to observe this instruction may cause damage to the overhead fittings and to the substation plant.

To regain speed after passing a section insulator with the trolleybus travelling over 15 m.p.h. the power pedal should be depressed at once to its full extent, provided the general traffic conditions permit.

48. *Always keep the overhead on the offside of the bus when turning corners* - this was the golden rule if the "sticks" were to stay on the overhead wire. Chance to do otherwise after the traffic island was installed at the top of Station Road was not an option as 90 turns into Wellesley Road. Croydon High School for Boys looms through the mist behind. (Terry Russell)

49. This view of 87 in Wellesley Road is a favourite of John Price. Taken on 11th November 1958, it shows where the road was widened to allow a tramway passing loop to be installed back in 1926. This deviation was still there in 1996. (J.H.Price)

50. The grand building beside 86 is Spurgeon's Tabernacle. My Cub and Scout Troop, the 10th Croydon met in the basement and endured monthly Church Parades in this forbidding looking building. *Further up the Creek* is showing at the Davis Theatre in the town. (J.H.Price)

51. If a penny was left from the school dinner money, a trolleybus ride home from this Spurgeon's Bridge stop could be enjoyed. Another will be along in 8 minutes! Through the trees lies the world renowned Gillett & Johnson's bell foundry. RT 4672 on the Saturday extension of the 159 poaches would be trolley riders before turning right and following the old, pre 1926 Oakfield Road tram route to West Croydon. (Terry Russell)

52. Long, straight, Whitehorse Road sees a Sutton bound trolleybus passing the Croydon Corporation children's nursery centre on its left, where my wife had her first job. (Terry Russell)

53. Local shops in Whitehorse Road included the grocers Home and Colonial and Stewarts, a tobacconist/barber owned by my Grandparents (before the Reeve's Corner employ). No.85 heads a cavalcade of London's public transport - in those days all operated by the same owner! (C.Carter)

54. The Gloster public house on the right, at the junction of Whitehorse, Windmill and Northcote Roads was bombed flat in 1944 along with nearby Luxor cinema. Neither opened their doors again after that raid, but the hostelry was rebuilt after this 1958 shot of 78 was taken. (D.Norman)

56. Lobb's Corner was another local name for this point arising from the newsagents ahead of 85, which is chasing an RT on the 75 route bound for Woolwich Free Ferry. It will continue to do so until the Robin Hood at Penge is reached. (Terry Russell)

55. On a snowy day, 70 waits to turn into Northcote Road on its way to Crystal Palace. Throughout the 1939-45 war traffic lights were masked as a blackout precaution. When they were removed it was a surprise to see that the lenses were inscribed STOP and GO. (Terry Russell)

SELHURST

57. I lived with my parents in Guildford Road, just off to the left, and remember the tram track being removed for "The War Effort". Steel was required and could not be left disused in the road. Here LT tram 49S, using the newly erected trolleybus overhead, waits at a Northcote Road passing loop for the car that Mr Masterman is riding. (E.G.P.Masterman)

58. At the same spot as the previous picture, brand new 79 pulls up at "my stop" in 1936. A young ear pressed to the pole could detect a trolley leaving Selhurst station.
(London Transport Museum)

59. Power to the trolleybus overhead was fed into isolated sections every half mile. The feeder point just east of the White Horse in Northcote Road was most troublesome. The overhead linesmen from Sutton depot in their Guy breakdown tender were often there. The driver of Croydon bound 86 will have coasted across the section breaker, taking no power, to avoid a 550 volt DC arc. (Terry Russell)

60. The headroom under the railway bridge in Selhurst Road was very restricted. The roadway was lowered to allow open top trams to pass under, but this left only minimal clearance for the full height trolleybuses with their roof mounted power collection gear. No.67 slowly approaches the Croydon side in March 1951. The dip in the road under the bridge was prone to flooding, hence the arrival of the class J3s in 1958. (J.H.Price)

878.—WEST CROYDON—CRYSTAL PALACE ROUTE.

Notice to Drivers and Conductors.

Until tramcars are replaced by trolleybuses on the above route the following instructions must be strictly observed.

Selhurst Station Bridge.
Penge Road Bridge (Selby Road).

Drivers must bring their cars to a standstill before passing under these bridges, in either direction.

Before giving signal to drivers, conductors must proceed to the upper deck and warn passengers to remain seated Whilst passing under the bridge the conductor must remain on the staircase in such a position that he can see tha passengers observe the instruction.

If men are working under the bridges conductors must ascertain from the linesman if it is safe to proceed befor giving the signal to drivers.

From LT traffic circular February 1936

61. Selhurst Station was adjacent to the bridge and 65 approaches the stop in Southern Electric days. The salt advertisment reminds us of Philip Harben's cookery programmes watched on a 9 inch, black and white television screen! (D.A.Thompson)

62. Platform 1 of Selhurst station spanned the bridge, so a one old penny platform ticket was a popular purchase. As 80 sets off for Croydon, we see a new electric EMU train in the siding of the railway repair works. This land was the original Selhurst Park football ground of the Crystal Palace FC and behind the far wall was my Father's allotment. Many hours were spent here during the early 1940s while Dad toiled at plot 275 and Terry sat on the wall watching the trains. (Terry Russell)

63. No.88 is in trouble in Selhurst Road, awaiting the Sutton breakdown tender. A nice day for walking the horse too! (Terry Russell)

1972.—TROLLEYBUS WINDSCREENS.

Notice to Trolleybus Drivers.

On account of the number of collisions with other buses, the front windscreens must not be opened more than the second notch, approximately 8 inches.

From LT traffic circular August 1938

64. Cause of the problem was the Ford Popular driver who tried to turn across 88 into the petrol filling station and lost! The front louvred panel has been removed to expose the towing hook. (Terry Russell)

65. The last Saturday of the 654s was dry and sunny, and 78 on its way to Croydon passes an RT bus on the 75s in South Norwood High Street. On the right is Norwood Clock Tower. *Erected by public subscription by the inhabitants of South Norwood to commemorate the Golden Wedding of Mr & Mrs W.F.Stanley of Cumberlow, South Norwood. February 22nd 1907.* - reads the inscription at its base. It remains a delightful landmark to this day. (Terry Russell)

66. One of the loaned class J3s is seen in South Norwood, High Street. Not much road space competition for 1051. Motorcycles with a sidecar fitted were popular as they could be driven on a motorcycle licence, but could convey the average small family - Dad, Mum and two half fares. (T.M.Russell Coll.)

67. Sutton bound 83 waits for the green light at the High Street/Portland Road crossing in May 1948. (J.H.Price)

68. No.92 turns on to Goat House Bridge across the main London Bridge to Croydon rail line. Between the overhead wires a string of light bulbs can be seen. Thick fogs often occurred in the winters of the past, and these lights were switched on to guide the trolleybus drivers. They were controlled by LT staff from the box on the right hand traction pole. On the left is the glass tower of the erstwhile Astoria cinema, closed in July 1957. (Terry Russell)

Operating Trolleybuses in Service

To ensure smooth acceleration when starting, Drivers should depress the power pedal sufficiently to apply one notch of power before releasing the hand brake and should then build up gradually.

If a trolleybus is accelerated too quickly the contactors will drop out, thus cutting off power. It is then necessary to return the power pedal to the "off" position and notch up afresh.

To decrease the speed of the trolleybus when travelling at a speed exceeding 15 m.p.h. the power pedal should be allowed to rise gradually. At speeds below 15 m.p.h. and in all cases of emergency the brake pedal must be used.

[NOTE.—The method of operation of the run-back brake and the electric coasting brake fitted to trolleybuses operating on Anerley Hill and Highgate Hill is dealt with under special instructions.]

After bringing the trolleybus to a standstill at a stopping place or in a line of traffic, the hand brake must always be applied and the brake pedal gradually released. Every endeavour must be made to stop as smoothly as circumstances will permit in order to avoid unpleasant jolting and possible skidding.

PENGE

69. The public house on the right was The Goat House. No.81, with a set of Charlton destination blinds, waits for the conductor's starting signal. (LTPS)

70. Trolley 79 must be early and taking it easy, or the motorcyclist would not have passed on the rise in Penge Road. (Terry Russell)

71. Roadworks in Penge Road cause 91 to swing to the wrong side of the road with trolleys at full stretch, while I was the subject of much youthful interest at the temporary stop sign. (Terry Russell)

72. Too fast under Selby Road bridge spelt disaster for 68! The trolleypoles dewired under the bridge, flew up under spring pressure and hit the metal girders. The repair gang have the job well in hand. Using a device called a "Jim Crow" they straighten the tubular steel booms before wrapping them with electrical insulation tape. The flailing booms also dislodged the plastic streetlight cover which the driver took home as a goldfish bowl! True... I was there! (Terry Russell)

73. In 1934 London Transport built experimental trolleybus 62 which was to be the prototype for all the fleet. It is seen on trial at the Robin Hood in Anerley in 1935. Close examination reveals that 62 has only one trolleypole up, on the single positive tramway overhead wire. The return current is through a heavy metal skate placed in tramway track on the end of a heavy chain. (F.Merton Atkins)

74. Ex SMET tram 50S turns from Croydon Road into Anerley Road on its way to Crystal Palace, taking its power from the inner positive trolleybus overhead wire. The outer wire is the trolleybus return, missing in the previous picture. The impressive frontage of Holy Trinity Church on the left was not to survive the 1939-45 war. (E.G.P.Masterman)

75. A spectacular, but less damaging dewirement happened to 79, right in front of Roy Hubble. I bet the driver of the 75 bus is highly amused. Beside the traction pole, also carrying the traffic signal, is a paraffin filled fog flair - a metal can with a wick filled spout which was lit when the "peasouper" fogs, caused by burning coal on household fires, descended. (R.Hubble)

ANERLEY

76. Early in 1936 at the first stop in Anerley Road, 69 picks up passengers. An inspector has a word with the driver who has two opening front windows to his bus. As built, these vehicles had a bench seat over the nearside front wheel. Distraction of the driver was probably the reason for it being replaced by a full width bulkhead.
(London Transport Museum)

77. A sylvan scene in Anerley! 78 has the road to itself on the next to last day. I drove this bus on battery power in Sutton Depot yard, so it holds a special affection. (R.Hubble)

78. On Anerley railway station bridge, 76 passes the local estate agents office while 90 loads for the Palace. The sign surmounted by a triangle warns road users of a crossing for school children ahead. The unusual front adverts were just to fill untaken space. The railway line is featured in Middleton Press album *London Bridge to East Croydon.* (J.H.Price)

79. Racing along Anerley Road, the driver of 90 overtakes a young man on his drop-handle bicycle who is clutching a bunch of flowers for a loved one. The Bond Minicar parked on the left, being a 3 wheeler, could also be driven on a Motorcycle Licence. The road from Robin Hood to the Palace was the only section of the route this side of Croydon, not shared by diesel buses. (J.H.Price)

80. At the point called ANERLEY ROBIN HOOD on the indicator blind, there was a turn back triangle. It was only used regularly on Saturday afternoons by one journey. No.84 backs from Anerley Road into Versailles Road for the last time, while the conductor keeps a good look out! (Terry Russell)

81. A view from Versailles road, across Anerley Road to Thicket Road shows the overhead layout perfectly. No.68 is scheduled to complete the full journey. The only other two reversing triangles on the London system are illustrated in companion volume *Woolwich and Dartford Trolleybuses*. (J.H.Price)

82. This odd operation continued up to the last Saturday of the service. No.84 completes the manoeuver by pulling out into Anerley Road to return to Sutton Depot. (Terry Russell)

CRYSTAL PALACE

927.—ROUTE No. 654—WEST CROYDON TO CRYSTAL PALACE SECTION.

Notice to Trolleybus Drivers and Conductors.

MINISTRY OF TRANSPORT REGULATIONS.

SPEED.

The following maximum speed limits must not be exceeded :—

30 *miles per hour.*
   In Croydon Road and Anerley Road between Selby Road bridge and Penge Town Hall.

20 *miles per hour.*
   In Wellesley Road and Whitehorse Road, Croydon.
   In High Street, South Norwood.

10 *miles per hour.*
   While crossing Goat House Bridge in both directions.
   While descending Anerley Hill from the top to Brunswick Place.

5 *miles per hour.*
   When rounding all turning circles and when passing under junctions or crossings in the overhead work, and under railway over-bridges.

   At all other places the speed must not exceed 25 *miles an hour.*

COMPULSORY STOPPING PLACES.

(1) At the top of Anerley Hill before commencing the descent, in order that the coasting brake may be switched on.
(2) On Anerley Hill opposite Tower Hall, at Pole No. 120 (head stop).
(3) On Anerley Hill before reaching Brunswick Place, in order that the coasting brake may be switched off.

STANDING PASSENGERS.

   No passengers may be permitted to stand while descending Anerley Hill, between the top of the hill and Brunswick Place.

From LT traffic circular March 1936

← 83. LAST BEFORE CRYSTAL PALACE states the addition to the stop sign at the bottom of Anerley Hill. Regulations decreed - no stopping on this steep incline for 492 on the upward journey. (LTPS)

← 84. No.68 on special duties passes Hamlet Road and the Low Level shopping parade. Anerley Hill can be seen rising in the background. Notley's are selling Esso Blue and Aladdin Pink paraffin oil, popular before the advent of central heating. (J.H.Price)

85. During the Board of Trade inspection in 1936 the specially fitted run-back prevention brake was tested by dewiring 65 and releasing the handbrake. As it did not run out of control to the bottom of the hill, public service commenced forthwith. The distinctive *Trolleybus* motif on the rear panel later became double sided and was moved up on to the window glass. The smaller version to the left of the entrance was discontinued in 1953, but the Sutton Depot painter carried stock to the end and so a set was preserved. Good old filmshow! (London Transport Museum)

86. Climbing the hill on the last Saturday, 493 still looks in good shape. Next week diesel fumes will fill the air, but 30 years ago few worried about this health hazard. (J.H.Price)

From LT traffic circular January 1943

87. Class B1 Trolleys had runaway prevention when running forward too! 69 stops at the compulsory Board of Trade stop midway down Anerley Hill. (Terry Russell)

Standing Passengers— Anerley Hill
3140

Staff on Route 654 are notified that the Regional Transport Commissioner has now rescinded the restriction on the number of passengers carried in trolleybuses whilst descending Anerley Hill. The normal regulations as to standing passengers, therefore, apply to this route, namely:—

" That between the hours of midnight and 7.30 p.m. the number of standing passengers which may be carried may not exceed one half of the number of passengers for which the vehicle has seating capacity on the lower deck, or 12, whichever is the less."

88. Before the age of the mass household telephone, kerbside fire alarms connected the caller direct to the local fire station. Ex SMET tram 49S makes one of its final runs under the new trolleybus overhead. The tower contained water tanks to supply the fountains in the grounds of the Crystal Palace. After the Palace was accidentally burnt down on the night of 30th November 1936, only this tower and its twin would remain. These too were demolished in the 1940s as they provided excellent landmarks for German aircraft. (A.D.Packer)

89. Only one bus was allowed at the final alighting stop at the Palace. No.70 along with 68 and 88 were fitted with aerials above the roof mounted suppressor coils. This was connected with another unsuccessful attempt to control overhead points from the cab. The "Torpedo" sidelights have been fitted at waist rail height, while the cantrail ones have not been panelled over. This bus has a set of Aldenham indicator blinds, which had thinner typeface than the Charlton product and never did look quite right! (A.B.Cross)

1594.—ROUTE No. 654—STOPPING PLACE—CRYSTAL PALACE.

Notice to Inspectors, Drivers and Conductors.

The stop on Pole No. 9, Anerley Hill, before passing round the turning circle, must be observed as a HEAD stop.

Drivers should endeavour to keep clear of the entrance to the Robin Wood Garage, and keep a sharp look-out for vehicles entering and leaving.

From LT traffic circular October 1937

90. A 1936 view with two new trolleybuses and the massive tower behind. Only the building disappeared, very little else changed during the trolleybus era. (J.H.Price Coll.)

91. The roundabout built as the trolleybus turning circle at the end of Crystal Palace Parade was a very modern idea in 1936. Its location at this junction of municipal boundaries involved the LCC, Kent and Surrey, but the newly created London Passenger Transport Board had the powers to over-ride any objections. (R.J.Harley Coll.)

92. Another favourite seat was lower saloon, front nearside, where the bench seat was originally situated. This view from 67 shows a well loaded coal lorry preparing to descend Anerley Hill, and 86 approaching the ALL CHANGE stop. Should the brake air pressure drop below a safe level, a red flag with STOP in silhouette would pop up from the cylinder below the centre pillar. (R.Hubble)

93. Our final shot of the Crystal Palace terminus, is a typical scene showing 80 on the stand. Although not visible, there is a large wooden block called a "Scotch" in front of the nearside, centre wheel, to prevent a runaway while the crew have a well earned tea break. The roadside sign warns of the dangerously steep, 1 in 10, (10%) hill. (R.Hubble)

94. Back in Carshalton depot yard on Tuesday, 3rd March 1959, the staff have made an effort by washing 65 for the last run with local dignitaries aboard later that night. No.64 was the first of the batch, but as it had been scrapped in 1955, they picked the next one. Tomorrow this crew, in their route 154 bus, will travel beyond Sutton Green to Morden. The Crystal Palace terminus remained unaltered. (T.M.Russell coll.)

95. Trolley 83 was the last "Rounder" and is seen here at Crystal Palace. The enthusiasts have put up EXTRA ready for the very last run by this clean, smooth mode of bygone public transport. To ensure that 83 would be THE LAST 654, our driver "hid" just short of the depot until 65, carrying local dignitaries had entered and only then did he arrive from Bushey Road, thus ensuring that the faithful enthusiasts were on the very last 654. (D.Norman)

Ten poles to stay

CROYDON is to keep a reminder of the former 654 trolley-bus route—now operated by diesel buses.

Croydon Council have informed London Transport that they wish to retain ten of the hundreds of poles supporting the overhead electric wires.

The poles will be used for direction signs and lighting standards.

London Transport are to make a "nominal charge" of one guinea for each pole.

96. After 83 had passed, the overhead linesmen got to work with indecent haste at West Croydon and Reeve's Corner removing all conflicting overhead fittings, thus giving the remaining 630 trolleys a hazard free run through Croydon. The next points they would have to negotiate in future, would be at Fair Green Mitcham and Tooting Broadway. (Terry Russell)

97. On 4th March 1959 all the remaining "Shorties" were driven away to the scrapyard at Colindale Depot. How untidy 86 looks with the front grill removed. The driver does not care anymore, and keeps the power on through the overhead point. This causes a large, damaging electrical arc, but its all over now, everything is just scrap metal...... (R.J.Harley Coll.)

98. One last look at a trio of B1s including 83 and 75, passing through Mitcham, on their way to be scrapped at Colindale. All the destination blinds were left piled up in Carshalton depot to be burnt by order of L T. Two sets were preserved by your author. Good old filmshow! (R.J.Harley Coll.)

Route 630 West Croydon to Mitcham

WEST CROYDON

99. Passengers wait at the 654 stop, while class K2, 1176 with the original unhelpful NR WILLESDEN JUNCTION destination, occupies the West Croydon stand in Station Road. Class D3, 544 eases out of the turning circle on one of London's longest trolleybus routes - 77 minutes to Scrubs Lane, Willesden. The driver of the front bus climbs into his cab to move forward as things are getting rather crowded. The bus with no rear indicator, a green, lowbridge type STL, is a stranger to the Country area route 409 to Godstone. (LTPS)

NEW 7d. CHEAP RETURN ON ROUTE No. 630.

Notice to Inspectors and Conductors—Hammersmith Depot.

Commencing on **Tuesday, 2nd August, 1938,** a new 7d. cheap return ticket will be put into use on Route No. 630 for the journey West Croydon Station and Tooting Station. A specimen ticket is exhibited in the depot. Pending provision of the necessary space on the waybill, conductors will enter ticket numbers in the 2d. Railway through booking ticket column.

100. The only time that Sutton B1s strayed from the 654 route was at Christmas. No.490 waits alone on the 630 layover stand in Station Road, before making the run to Fair Green, Mitcham. This saved excessive dead mileage by the usual Hammersmith Depot vehicles. The route blind showed EXTRA as Sutton blinds did not contain 630. As the Mitcham turnback was not wired from the Croydon direction, the driver would continue to Figges Marsh, and back into Lavender Avenue using battery power to make the reversal. (R.J.Harley Coll.)

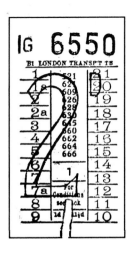

101. Class P1, 1702 has West Croydon to itself now the 654 has gone. An inexperienced driver might have needed a second bite at the tight turn, especially if a car was parked at the bottom of St Michael's Road. (L.Rowe)

102. An unusual vehicle is seen at West Croydon in 1948 in the shape of a class B2 without run back brake facility on the 630. Just why Hammersmith Depot should have a 60 seater in its allocation is a mystery. (G.E.Baddeley)

103. On a busy day, class F1, 658 enters Station Road after crossing the main road to London at West Croydon. The fine 1930s art-deco frontage of Stones, the electrical appliance supplier, provides an impressive backdrop. I remember buying thorn needles for Dad's gramophone at discount rate as "Old man Stone" was a family friend. (R.Hubble)

104. In happier times, when Reeve's Corner was served by both routes, class D3, 537 prepares to turn right from Tamworth Road into Lower Church Street in Old Town. The latter road was single line working for the 630s. The conductor set the overhead points at the control box on the traction pole supporting the stop signs, the driver would check the hooded indicator on the left pole for a "clear to enter" signal. Similarly, a Croydon bound bus would enter only after checking his signal if the section was clear. His presence was triggered by a skate switch in the overhead. The bus routes which used the stop with the shelter were shown in black on white enamel plates placed in slots beneath the main sign. (A.D.Packer)

105. The Trolleybuses had only three days of operation left before Stage 7 of the conversion, on this last Saturday, 16th July 1960. Class F1, 656 leaves Lower Church Street, while an RT on route 157 waits at the traffic lights at Reeve's Corner. The building behind was another early Croydon cinema. It had been the *Dome and Olympic* until 1916, before Messrs. Reeve bought the premises in 1927. (J.H.Price)

106. Class D2, 461 is waiting for the "all clear" to enter the single line section of Lower Church Street and once again electric traction rules. One dark, winter evening, my bus riding grandmother and I were turned off the 630 trolleybus at this point. It was no great hardship as we only had to walk round the corner and pick up the 654 home. I have often wondered why this happened. Was he running so late that rather than finish the final run up to West Croydon, he turned here on battery power? (Pamlin Prints)

From LT traffic circular September 1937

1560.—SIGNAL CONTROL SYSTEM—JUNCTION OF LOWER CHURCH STREET AND TAMWORTH ROAD, CROYDON.

TROLLEYBUS OPERATION.

At the junction of Lower Church Street and Tamworth Road, Croydon, a trolleybus must not be driven beyond the end of Lower Church Street towards Sutton, or enter Lower Church Street towards Mitcham, whilst a bus is proceeding out of Lower Church Street towards Croydon.

Signals controlling this junction are installed at Pole 246 in Tamworth Road and Pole 2 in Lower Church Street.

The frog at this junction is electrically operated.

Trolleybuses to Sutton and Mitcham must stop with head of bus opposite "push button" post, between Poles 245 and 246, unless the yellow signal or the arrow head signal is showing.

The frog is automatically set for the curve into Lower Church Street, and buses for Sutton must set frog for the "Straight" road by operating push button on post between poles 245 and 246. This button must not be operated whilst a bus is on the "Down" track between this post and the frog.

There is an emergency button for setting the frog for the "BRANCH" road if for any reason this has not been done automatically.

Trolleybuses travelling from Mitcham towards Croydon must not leave the stop at Pole 4 until the yellow signal or the arrow head signal is showing.

The yellow lights indicate that there is no bus either passing the end of Lower Church Street or leaving or entering it.

The horizontal signal indicates that a bus is coming towards signal in opposite direction (STOP). The vertical arrows show that a bus is ahead in same direction (other buses can follow).

Straight and Angle arrow heads at Pole 246 show whether frog is set for the "STRAIGHT" or the "BRANCH" (CURVE).

107. On the northern approach to Pitlake Bridge, class K1, 1119, brought in to replace the ageing class Ds, nears the end of the run from north of the Thames in March 1960. (Pamlin Prints)

108. Leaving Mitcham Road just past the Army barracks, class D2, 449 swings on to the wrong side of the carriageway to avoid some road resurfacing work. Trolleybuses were not so inflexible as their critics would have us believe. Traffic patterns in those days remained static for many years, and the vehicles carried traction batteries of the type used on the milk floats of 1996. Trolleybuses were thus able to run at low speed, away from the overhead supply. (Terry Russell)

109. The rural run along Croydon Road across Mitcham Common was a trolleybus driver's dream, quite straight, and few stops. Class F1, 743 races towards Mitcham, Tooting, Putney, Hammersmith, Shepherds Bush and finally Harlesden during the last week of operation. We can deduce the date by the yellow notices on the traction poles informing the public that, after Tuesday next, they will be travelling on the all conquering Routemaster bus on route 220, or an older RT on route 64. (A.B.Cross)

2180
Route No. 630— Easter Monday

Notice to Inspectors and Conductors, Hammersmith Depot.

On Easter Monday certain Route No. 630 trolleybuses will operate from Hanwell Depot, but will be manned by staff from Hammersmith Depot.

Route No. 655 tickets will be supplied for use when running between Hanwell Depot and Hammersmith Broadway and Route No. 630 tickets for use during the service journeys.

Destination Blinds. The following wording must be shown :—

When Running to	Front and Rear	Side Blind
West Croydon	13 via Putney & Tooting	Croydon
Scrubs Lane	12 Nr. Willesden Junction via Putney	Mitcham, 4 Tooting, Putney, Hammersmith
Hammersmith	3 Hammersmith Broadway	
Hanwell Depot	1 Private	

From LT traffic circular 1939

110. On Whitsun Bank Holiday Monday in 1950, at the Ravensbury Arms on Mitcham Common, there is a stranger in the camp. This picture was taken before the roundabout in the following photograph was built. Class F1, 750, running out of Hanwell depot is supplementing the 630 service, displaying a 3x running number on the side. (J.H.Meredith)

111. With a convoy of private cars behind, class K1, 1075 enters the roundabout at the junction of Croydon Road with Commonside West and Carshalton Road on 26th June 1960. All the advertisements are for the "Demon Drink", which was so often the case in later years. As we have now left the Croydon area, this is a convenient place to end our tour of the trolleybus routes of Croydon. (L.Rowe).

630 FINALE

112. Our final picture, was taken in the late evening of Tuesday, 19th July 1960, on the occasion of the very last trolleybus to run in Croydon. The "Rogues Gallery" of enthusiasts have left their individual modes of transport at Hammersmith, and boarded class K1, 1121 for the last run to West Croydon and return. Derek Norman is recording and Mike Skeggs is in the crowd, both of whom have contributed photographs to this volume. The reason for the rear of the bus being chosen for this shot, is that the front indicator blinds were missing. The long parcel is held by a rather youthful looking Terry Russell. Despite the occasion, the inspector on the right refused to allow the enthusiasts to ride round the turning circle, and made us walk up Station Road to the correct boarding point and wait for 1121 to arrive. (T.M.Russell Coll.)

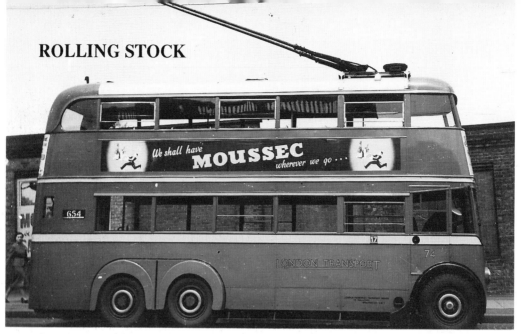

113. Class B1, 64-93 built by Birmingham Railway, Carriage & Wagon Co. on 16ft.6ins./5029mm wheelbase chassis. Delivered: November 1935 to January 1936. Seating: 32 upper deck, 28 lower deck. This was reduced to 26 when a full bulkhead was fitted behind the driver in 1938. Livery: red with cream bands and black lines between colours. Roof: gloss red ends with silver centre section. Features: offside rear route stencil holder and conductors window, single white on black enamel running number on the waist rail. Sidelights were let into the cantrail above the drivers front window. Both front and rear panels beside the indicators carried advertisements. Deep, red painted metal mud shields over the rear wheels, which were later cut back to facilitate easier wheel removal, put the finishing touch to a very fine, pollution free, electric public carrier. (J.H.Price Coll.)

114. In March 1957, No.80 had just been overhauled and repainted in the traditional trolleybus livery, with none of the labour saving schemes that were being tried on the diesel bus fleet at that time. Very little has changed in 21 years, the roof is now painted with a gloss red front dome, matt brown centre section and gloss brown rear dome. The rear offside, sliding window and stencil holder are out of use, and have been removed from many of the class. The cantrail sidelights were replaced by the "Torpedo" type below the waistrail or the flush fitting style on the front panelling. The running number plate is now an aluminium stencil and has been expanded to include a garage code - CN for Carshalton and HB for Hammersmith. The owners details now only appear in white letters on the nearside front access panel. (R.Hubble)

115. Class B1, 489-493 built by BRCW and delivered in September 1936. A near identical batch, the differences were: rubber rear wheel mud shields and no conductors window. They were subjected to all the same modifications as the original batch, but retained the nearside front opening window. I have always thought that it was nigh impossible for the conductor to give hand signals using the offside rear, sliding window - hence its omission from the later batches. If, as it has been suggested, it was to illuminate the staircase, then why was it sliding and not fixed? Conductors had white cuff bands on their jacket sleeves, as they were expected to assist the driver by giving hand direction signals to other road users from the rear platform, in addition to all their other duties. (A.B.Cross)

116. Class D2, 385-483 delivered in December 1936, on 18ft.7ins./5672mm chassis built by Metro-Cammell. No.445, a typical 630 vehicle for many years working from Hammersmith Depot, is seen turning at West Croydon. These buses were built with a full width bulkhead behind the driver. (C.Carter).

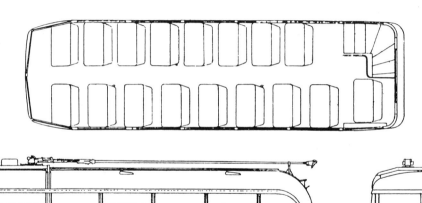

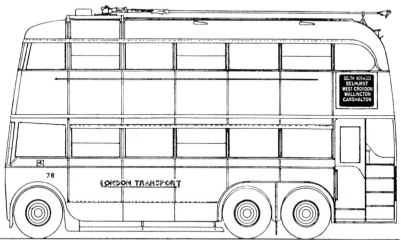

654

CRYSTAL PALACE
via CROYDON
& SOUTH NORWOOD

SOUTH NORWOOD
SELHURST
WEST CROYDON
WALLINGTON
CARSHALTON

78

LONDON TRANSPORT

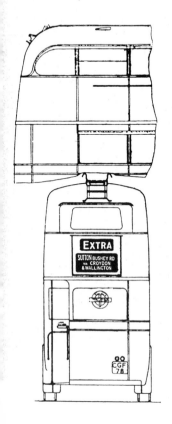

EXTRA

SUTTON BUSHEY RD
via CROYDON
& WALLINGTON

CGF
78

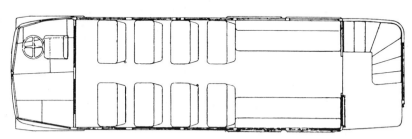

LONDON TRANSPORT TROLLEYBUS	
SHORT WHEELBASE 60 SEAT	
BUILT: B.R.C & W. 1935 CLASS: B1. NO. 64 - 93.	SCALE: 4 MM = 1 FOOT
DRAWING No. TB 1	

SCALE
FEET   0 1 2 3 4 5 6 7 8 9 10 11 12

DRAWN BY:- TERRY RUSSELL, "CHACESIDE", ST.LEONARDS PARK, HORSHAM, W.SUSSEX. RH13 6EG.
SEND 3 FIRST CLASS STAMPS FOR COMPLETE LIST OF PUBLIC TRANSPORT DRAWINGS.

Flooded Roadway

Trolleybuses must not be driven upon flooded roads at a speed exceeding 5 m.p.h. and must be kept as far as possible on the crown of the road. In no circumstances must trolleybuses be driven upon a flooded road if the level of water is above the bottom edge of the lifeguard slat.

117. Class J3, 1030-1054, delivered by BRCW in November 1938. Seen here is 1049 loaned to Sutton depot in 1948, while their flooded B1s were dried out. (M.Skeggs Coll.)

118. Class H1, 755-904 delivered in February 1938 by Metro-Cammell, and class P1, 1697-1721 delivered by the same firm in February 1941. After route 654 had been converted to diesel bus, we see two 630 trolleybuses at West Croydon. On the left 1700 is on the layover stand, while 780 pulls out on its way to Harlesden. These two seem to have a crossed indicator problem. A horizontal, circular wave of the hand to the driver would get the message across. At the next stop he would alert the conductor, who would go upstairs and using a special key, release the complete display (hinged at the bottom), and rest it against the front seats for destination blind alteration. (LTPS)

119. In the early days of trolleybus operation, the overhead wires were coated with a graphite varnish using a fascinating vehicle, No. 41H in the service fleet. Beneath the smooth 1930s panelling is ex LGOC omnibus NS 760. It saw service from 1936 to 1940, after which improved carbon trolleyhead inserts made it redundant. It ran independently of the over-

continued ➔

head power supply, using its original petrol bus engine, while the trolleyheads applied the lubricant from partially immersed wheels. These photographs were taken by one of the crew of the "Greaser" in 1936. New style LPTB stop signs can be seen on the traction pole behind. The open window above the driver enabled him to follow the overhead more accurately than would normally be required. (T.M.Russell Coll.)

120. A close up shot of the radiator of 41H, reveals its original owner, with GENERAL on the header tank. (T.M.Russell Coll.)

MP Middleton Press

Easebourne Lane, Midhurst. West Sussex. GU29 9AZ   Tel: 01730 813169 Fax: 01730 812601
. . . . . Write or telephone for our latest list . . . . .

BRANCH LINES

Branch Line to Allhallows
Branch Lines to Alton
Branch Lines around Ascot
Branch Line to Bude
Branch Lines around Canterbury
Branch Lines to East Grinstead
Branch Lines around Effingham Jn
Branch Lines to Exmouth
Branch Line to Fairford
Branch Line to Hawkhurst
Branch Lines to Horsham
Branch Lines around Huntingdon
Branch Lines to Ilfracombe
Branch Line to Lyme Regis
Branch Line to Lynton
Branch Lines around March
Branch Lines around Midhurst
Branch Lines to Newport
Branch Line to Padstow
Branch Lines around Portmadoc 1923-46
Branch Lines around Porthmadog 1954-94
Branch Lines to Seaton & Sidmouth
Branch Line to Selsey
Branch Lines around Sheerness
Branch Line to Southwold
Branch Line to Swanage
Branch Line to Tenterden
Branch Lines to Torrington
Branch Lines to Tunbridge Wells
Branch Line to Upwell
Branch Lines around Weymouth

LONDON SUBURBAN RAILWAYS

Caterham and Tattenham Corner
Clapham Jn. to Beckenham Jn.
Crystal Palace and Catford Loop
Holborn Viaduct to Lewisham
London Bridge to Addiscombe
Mitcham Junction Lines
South London Line
West Croydon to Epsom
Willesden Junction to Richmond
Wimbledon to Epsom

STEAMING THROUGH

Steaming through Cornwall
Steaming through East Sussex
Steaming through the Isle of Wight
Steaming through Surrey
Steaming through West Hants
Steaming through West Sussex

GREAT RAILWAY ERAS

Ashford from Steam to Eurostar
Festiniog in the Fifties

COUNTRY BOOKS

Brickmaking in Sussex
East Grinstead Then and Now

SOUTH COAST RAILWAYS

Ashford to Dover
Bournemouth to Weymouth
Brighton to Eastbourne
Brighton to Worthing
Chichester to Portsmouth
Dover to Ramsgate
Hastings to Ashford
Ryde to Ventnor
Worthing to Chichester

SOUTHERN MAIN LINES

Bromley South to Rochester
Charing Cross to Orpington
Crawley to Littlehampton
Dartford to Sittingbourne
East Croydon to Three Bridges
Epsom to Horsham
Exeter to Barnstaple
Exeter to Tavistock
Faversham to Dover
Haywards Heath to Seaford
London Bridge to East Croydon
Orpington to Tonbridge
Sittingbourne to Ramsgate
Swanley to Ashford
Three Bridges to Brighton
Tonbridge to Hastings
Victoria to Bromley South
Waterloo to Windsor
Woking to Southampton
Yeovil to Exeter

COUNTRY RAILWAY ROUTES

Andover to Southampton
Bath to Evercreech Junction
Bournemouth to Evercreech Jn
Burnham to Evercreech Junction
Croydon to East Grinstead
East Kent Light Railway
Fareham to Salisbury
Guildford to Redhill
Porthmadog to Blaenau
Reading to Basingstoke
Reading to Guildford
Redhill to Ashford
Salisbury to Westbury
Strood to Paddock Wood
Taunton to Barnstaple
Westbury to Bath
Woking to Alton

TROLLEYBUS CLASSICS

Croydon's Trolleybuses
Woolwich & Dartford Trolleybuses

TRAMWAY CLASSICS

Aldgate & Stepney Tramways
Bournemouth & Poole Tramways
Brighton's Tramways
Bristol's Tramways
Camberwell & W. Norwood Tramway
Croydon's Tramways
Dover's Tramways
East Ham & West Ham Tramways
Embankment & Waterloo Tramways
Exeter & Taunton Tramways
Greenwich & Dartford Tramways
Hampstead & Highgate Tramways
Hastings Tramways
Ilford & Barking Tramways
Kingston & Wimbledon Tramways
Lewisham & Catford Tramways
Maidstone & Chatham Tramways
North Kent Tramways
Portsmouth's Tramways
Southampton Tramways
Southend-on-sea Tramways
Thanet's Tramways
Victoria & Lambeth Tramways
Walthamstow & Leyton Tramways
Wandsworth & Battersea Tramways

OTHER RAILWAY BOOKS

Garraway Father & Son
Industrial Railways of the South East
London Chatham & Dover Railway
South Eastern Railway
War on the Line

MILITARY BOOKS

Battle over Portsmouth
Battle Over Sussex 1940
Blitz Over Sussex 1941-42
Bognor at War
Bombers over Sussex 1943-45
Military Defence of West Sussex

WATERWAY ALBUMS

Hampshire Waterways
Kent and East Sussex Waterways
London to Portsmouth Waterway
West Sussex Waterways

BUS BOOK

Eastbourne Bus Story

SOUTHERN RAILWAY
● VIDEOS ●

Memories of the Hayling Island Branch
Memories of the Lyme Regis Branch
War on the Line